Kah'Lonee'
SUNNY DAYS RECIPES

KAH'LONEE' PRYOR

About the Author

Hi, My name is Kah'Lonee' Pryor. I will be eight years old on October 25, 2018. I am currently in the Second grade! I was born in 2010 in the state of California. I love eating Pizza, Sushi, Crab and Shrimp. My hobbies are Singing, Reading, Acting, Modeling, Ballet Dancing, Ballroom Dancing, Hip-Hop Dancing, Gymnastics, Tumbling, Poetry, Creative Inventing, Martial Arts, Exercising, playing the Guitar, Violin, Saxophone, Flute, Piano, Harmonica and Trombone. When I grow up, I want to become a Make-Up Artist, Fashion Designer, Singer, Model, Actress, Poet, Gymnast, Inventor, Business Investor, Realtor, Personal Fitness Trainer, Yoga Instructor and continue on being a successful Author! My Parents, my big Brother, my Uncles, and Grand Parents are my supporter's and motivator's. I love my Parents, I love my Grandparents, I love my Family, I love my Brother and the rest of my Siblings. I love being a kid, making people smile and laugh and making new friends. In the past, I have attended Martial Arts, Commercial Modeling, Acting Classes, Tumbling and Gymnastics. I've been awarded plenty of Trophies, Certificates, and Rewards, but my major accomplishment was being the most advanced student in my first grade class; solving Math Problems at a fourth grade level. I'm very proud and excited for my brother, Dai'Jon Pryor, on having his Children's Book called, Look Inside and his Coloring Book called, DP Arts Coloring Book both published. I'm currently working on creating my own Lip Gloss, Lotion, and Fashion Line. With this all being shared, hopefully reader's will enjoy my Recipe Book full of interesting and creative Recipes. Have an open mind, have fun being a kid, lean towards higher learning and always believe in yourself. I personally, want to give praise to God for all of my blessing's, talent's, gift's and strength. Next, I want to give much appreciation to my Mommy who is loving, caring, beautiful, strong, educated, and the best Mommy ever! Lastly, I'll like to dedicate this book to my Father!

About the Book

This recipe book was designed to share creative recipes to help with making smoothies, slushes, shakes, salads, snacks, desserts, and dinner dishes. If your heart is in the kitchen, share the love with others to help them experience, grow, and gain abundance of confidence. I hope my recipe book helps kids and adults build closer bonds while creating fun memories in the kitchen. Sharing is caring, so as you open your eyes to dive into Kah'Lonee's Sunny Days Recipes, I hope you find it in your heart to share with others your favorite recipes found within my recipe book. Enjoy and keep sharing blessings to the world!

To order additional copies of this book, contact:
Xlibris
844-714-8691
www.Xlibris.com
Orders@Xlibris.com

1) Uncle's Pepperoni Pizza Quesadilla

Wash your hands with soap and water for 30 seconds.

- Cut triangle shaped pieces from each Tortilla Shell
- Add (1) slice of Swiss Cheese on top of each triangle Tortilla Shell
- Add (2) Pepperoni slices on top of sliced Swiss Cheese
- Add a triangle Tortilla Shell on top of each triangle Tortilla Shell
- Fry each Shell on stove top in skillet with 1oz of Vegetable Oil
- Consistently rotate sides every 60 seconds
- Fry on medium-low heat and watch carefully

Enjoy! :-)

2) Sausage N Bacon

Wash your hands with soap and water for 30 seconds.

- Fry breakfast Maple Sausages on stove top in skillet with 1oz of Vegetable Oil
- Fry Bacon on stove top in skillet with 1oz of Vegetable Oil
- Chop Sausages and Bacon into pieces
- Preheat oven 300°
- Butter pan
- Split each uncooked Biscuit in half
- Sprinkle chopped Sausages, Bacon and shredded Swiss Cheese in the middle of each uncooked Biscuit
- Close each uncooked Biscuit
- Place each uncooked Biscuit onto oven pan
- Bake Biscuits in the oven until golden brown or desired
- May also use boiled Hot Dogs

Enjoy! :-)

3) Daddy Crab stuffed Lobster

Wash your hands with soap and water for 30 seconds.

- Preheat oven 300°
- Place greased pan inside of the oven
- Bake a Whole Potatoe and slightly cut in the center
- Bake until Whole Potatoe is soft
- Boil Crab Legs on stove top on high heat with one stick of Butter added
- May Season Crab Legs if desired with Lemon Pepper, Cayenne Pepper, Black Pepper and/or Seasoned Salt
- Boil Lobsters on stove top on high heat with one stick of Butter added
- May Season Lobsters if desired with Lemon Pepper, Black Pepper, Cayenne Pepper and/or Seasoned Salt
- Once Crab Legs, Lobsters and the Whole Potato are cooked well done
- Add 1oz of American/Swiss Cheese into the center of the baked Potato
- Add chopped Crab Meat and chopped Lobster Meat
- Place back into the oven for 3-7 minutes
- Let cool down on countertop for 2 minutes

Enjoy! :-)

4) Prince DJ Veggie Remix

Wash your hands with soap and water for 30 seconds.

- Add 4oz of fried String Beans on a skillet with 1oz of Vegetable Oil at medium heat on stove top
- Add 4oz of chopped cooked White Potatoes
- Add 2oz of chopped Green Onions
- Add 1 teaspoon of Black Pepper sprinkled on top
- Add 1 teaspoon of Seasoned Salt sprinkled on top
- Add 1oz of chopped Green, Yellow, Red & Orange Bell Peppers
- Add 4oz of fried Spinach in a skillet on stove top with 1oz of Vegetable Oil on medium heat
- Mix well for 10 seconds

Enjoy! :-)

5) Dai'Jon Spinach Rice Mix

Wash your hands with soap and water for 30 seconds.

- Add 16oz of fried Spinach
- Add 8oz of fried Bok Choy
- Add 2oz of fried chopped Orange, Green, Red & Yellow Bell Peppers
- Add (7) slices of fried than chopped Bacon
- Add 2oz of slightly fried chopped Green Onions
- Add (1) whole chopped and fried Cucumber
- Add (3) chopped boiled than fried Hot Dogs
- Add 8oz of White Sticky Rice with Butter flavour cooked in skillet on stove top at medium heat
- Add Spinach, Bok Choy, Bell Peppers, Bacon, Hot Dogs, Onions & Cucumbers on top of Rice

Enjoy! :-)

6) Salsa Shocker

Wash your hands with soap and water for 30 seconds.

- Add (1) large can of Pace the Original Picante Sauce {medium}
- Add (1) whole chopped White Onion
- Add 1oz of Dry Chopped Garlic
- Add (1) tablespoon of Onion Powder
- Add 1oz of Dill Relish
- Add 1oz of Minced Onions
- Add 1oz of shredded Swiss/American Cheese
- Add 1oz of Ranch Dressing
- Add 1oz of chopped Cilantro
- Add 1oz of chopped fried Spinach
- Add 1oz of chopped fried Orange, Yellow, Green & Red Bell Peppers
- Add (7) sliced fried chopped Bacon
- Add 1oz of cooked Black Beans or Kidney Beans
- Add 2oz of chopped fried Bok Choy
- Add 1oz of chopped Black Olives
- Add 8oz of cooked sticky White Rice with Butter flavor
- Mix altogether

Enjoy! :-)

7) Princess KK Meat Loaf Cupcakes

Wash your hands with soap and water for 30 seconds.

- Preheat oven 300°
- Slightly grease oven pan with Vegetable Oil
- Crack (3) Eggs into a cup & stir well until satisfied
- Pour Eggs into Ground Turkey/Beef
- Mix well for 30 seconds
- Design Meat as you please than put into the oven to bake for 60-90 minutes
- Cook Mash Potatoes in medium size pot on stove top at medium heat
- Use Butter and Seasoning if desired
- Once Meat Loaf & Mash Potatoes are cooked well done
- Cut out square pieces of Meat Loaf
- Use clean/new Scissors to cut out a small hole at the tip of the new big zip lock bag
- Squeeze Mash Potatoes on top of each Meat Loaf piece going in circle motion to make cupcake swirls

Enjoy! :-)

8) Wayne Supreme Fried Chicken

Wash your hands with soap and water for 30 seconds.

- Heat Vegetable Oil in cooking pot on stove top at medium heat
- Add (30) Party Wings of Chicken
- May dip into Seasoned Flour/Corn Meal
- Add 8oz of fried Jalapeno Peppers
- Add 4oz of fried Orange, Red, Green & Yellow Bell Peppers
- Add 4oz of chopped slightly fried Green Onions
- Mix the Jalapenos, all of the Bell Peppers and Green Onions altogether
- Pour on top of the Fried Chicken

Enjoy! :-)

9) Mom Variety Sweets

Wash your hands with soap and water for 30 seconds.

- Pancake with Chocolate or Carmel swirls on top
- Add (1) whole chopped Banana
- Add Whipped Cream
  Or you may desire:
- 1oz of Green Grapes
  Or you may desire:
- Cheesecake
- Add (1) whole Strawberry
- Add (2) slices of Mandarin Oranges

- Add (2) slices of Kiwi
  Or you may desire:
- Vanilla Chocolate Carmel Cheesecake
- Add (2) chopped Strawberries
- Add (3) Blueberries
- Add (3) Blackberries

Enjoy! :-)

10) NeNe variety Fruit

Wash your hands with soap and water for 30 seconds.

- Add 3oz of Grapes
- Add 3oz of Peaches
- Add 2oz of Strawberries
- Add 2oz of Bananas
- May also add Lettuce, Ugli Fruit, JuJube, Tangelo, Gooseberry, Papaya and Pomegranate
- Mix well for 10 seconds

Enjoy! :-)

11) Nana Zesty Salad Bang

Wash your hands with soap and water for 30 seconds.

- Add 8oz of chopped Green Leaf Lettuce
- Add 4oz of chopped Kale
- Add 4oz of chopped Spinach
- Add 2oz of Kraft Italian Zesty Salad Dressing
- Add 1oz of Ranch Dressing
- Add 1oz of chopped Tomatoes
- Add 1oz of chopped Cucumbers
- Add 1oz of chopped Green Onions
- Add 1oz of chopped Black Olives
- Add 1oz of chopped shredded Carrots
- Add 1oz of chopped Green, Yellow, Orange & Red Bell Peppers
- Add 1oz of shredded Swiss Cheese
- Add (1) Boiled Egg chopped well
- Add 1oz of cooked White Corn
- Add 1oz of cooked Cauliflower
- Add (1) can of Black Beans
- Add (1) can of Kidney Beans
- Mix well for 10 seconds
- Chop (1) half of Red Bell Pepper and chop (1) half of Yellow Bell Pepper
- Slightly fry each half of Bell Pepper on stove top in skillet with 1oz of Vegetable Oil at medium heat
- Melt American Cheese on top of each half
- Sprinkle chopped fried Green Onions, chopped fried Pepperoni pieces, and chopped fresh Tomatoes on top

Enjoy! :-)

12) Dathan Green Salad Mix

Wash your hands with soap and water for 30 seconds.

- Add 16oz of chopped Iceberg Head Lettuce
- Add 1oz of chopped Green Grapes
- Add (1) whole chopped Cucumber
- Add 2oz of chopped Green Bell Peppers
- Add 1oz of Garlic Powder
- Add (1) whole chopped Green Apple
- Add 2oz of chopped Green Onions
- Add 3oz of chopped Spinach
- Add 3oz of chopped Kale
- Add 2oz of chopped Celintro
- Add 4oz of Ranch Dressing
- Mix well for 10 seconds

Enjoy! :-)

13) Kah'Lonee' Taco Bowl

Wash your hands with soap and water for 30 seconds.

- Add 2oz of Green Leaf Lettuce
- Add 2oz of Ground Turkey/Beef/Steak cooked well done
- Add 1oz of Spinach
- Add 1oz of Kale
- Add 1oz of Ranch Dressing
- Add 1oz of chopped Tomatoes
- Add 1oz of chopped Cucumbers
- Add 1oz of chopped Green Onions
- Add 1oz of chopped Black Olives
- Add 1oz of chopped shredded Carrots
- Add 1oz of Green, Red, Yellow & Orange Bell Peppers
- Add 1oz of shredded Swiss Cheese
- Add 1oz of cooked White Corn
- Mix well for 10 seconds
- You may eat alone or add onto a Tortilla Shell

Enjoy! :-)

14) Honey Bun Sweet Tooth

Wash your hands with soap and water for 30 seconds.

- Preheat oven at 300°
- Butter Pan
- Place Honey Bun in center of pan
- Add Jelly Beans and Mott's onto Honey Bun
- Place Another Honey Bun on top to complete Sandwich
- Bake in oven for 17 minutes
- Let cool down on the countertop for 10 minutes
- May add Peanut Butter on top

Enjoy! :-)

15) Glamorous Sushi Dessert

Wash your hands with soap and water for 30 seconds.

- Add 2 cups of Sushi Rice
- Add 2 1/2 cups of Purified Water
- Add 4 tablespoons of Sugar
- Add 1/4 teaspoon of Salt
- Add 1 cup of Coconut Milk
- Add 1 teaspoon of Vanilla Extract
- Add 8oz of chopped Fruit pieces of your choice

Enjoy! :-)

16) Fantastic Back Flips

Wash your hands with soap and water for 30 seconds.

- Chop (1) whole Green Apple
- Add sliced Green Apples onto plate
- Chop (1) whole Banana
- Add chopped Banana slices onto the plate
- Add Strawberry Applesauce on top of each slice of Green Apple
- Add a Pretzel on top of each Banana slice

Enjoy! :-)

17) What's up Sweet N Sour Fruity Smoothie

Wash your hands with soap and water for 30 seconds.

- Add 8oz of Vanilla Ice Cream
- Add 2oz of Vitamin D Milk
- Add 8oz of crushed Ice
- Add (17) Skittles Candy
- Add (17) Sour Patches Candy
- Add (1) Banana
- Add (1) Red Vine
- Add (7) Strawberries
- Blend for 30-60 Seconds
- Add (2) sliced Pineapples
- Add (2) sliced Pears
- Add (2) sliced Oranges
- Add (2) Green Apples
- Blend for 30-90 seconds

Enjoy! :-)

18) Yikes- Love Yit Smoothie

Wash your hands with soap and water for 30 seconds.

- Add 4oz of crushed Ice
- Add 4oz of Blueberry Yogurt
- Add 1oz of Cranberry Cocktail 100% Juice
- Add (4) sliced Pineapples
- Add (4) sliced Green Apples
- Blend for 30 seconds
- Add (1) sliced Lemon
- Add (1) sliced Lime
- Add (1) sliced Kiwi
- Add (1) Banana
- Add (4) sliced Oranges
- Add (4) sliced Plums
- Add (7) sliced Green Apples
- Blend for 30-90 seconds

Enjoy! :-)

19) Pure Veggie Smoothie

Wash your hand switch soap and water for 30 seconds.

- Add 8oz of crushed Ice
- Add 8oz of Purified cold Water
- Add 1 tablespoon of Avocado
- Add 1oz of chopped Tomatoes
- Add 1/2 chopped Cucumber
- Add 1oz of chopped Broccoli
- Add 1oz of chopped Carrots
- Add 1oz of chopped Spinach
- Add 1oz of chopped Green Bell Peppers
- Blend for 30-90 seconds

Enjoy! :-)

20) Grandpa Smoothie

Wash your hands with soap and water for 30 seconds.

- Add 8oz of crushed Ice
- Add 8oz of 100% Orange Juice
- Add (7) Strawberries
- Add (7) sliced Pears
- Add (7) sliced Peaches
- Blend for 30 seconds
- Add (3) sliced Pineapples
- Add (2) sliced Green Apples
- Add (17) Green Grapes
- Add (1) Banana
- Add 1oz of chopped Carrots
- Blend for 30-90 seconds

Enjoy! :-)

Haiku

Shedding of betel –
Slackening! Ground it settle.
Soon, no one can tell!

Steep hill with warm mist,
Sound of mellifluent drift
Sad streams that flow swift.

The blue brightest sky –
Hides the compelling dark side.
Life offers surprise!

Blossom of the shade,
Rare exciting masquerade.
To the world: pervade!

Mystifying Moon,
Shining one late afternoon
Bay watch in mid-June.

Great waves leave no trace,
What else can sea-wave erase?
My hopes? Your embrace!

Clear spotless white wall,
Damn! Made me cry. Made me bawl.
Tears like waterfall.

Cold eerie soul's tune
Like a craterous red moon
No one asked for choon!

Shadows of the past
Through nightmares you do harassed
Don't know when will last.

Rocky niche plunge pool
Water flows swiftly like fool
Dazing drops cruel.

Child's tears-eyed laughter,
Mothers ultimate success!
Mix of emotion.

After the cold nights,
Here comes the flourishing buds.
What a change of scene!

Orange spot sunset,
Angry Tigress roaring pain,
Birth to a twin cubs.

Most feared Tornado,
Come visit me tomorrow!
Go! Shot more arrows!

Free Verse

Give it a leap of faith,
       a hurdle without hate.
Know that struggle is gate,
       not the pal on the fate.

You created me along with the rainbow
'though life was not all colors but more of sorrow.
You gave me Genesis 19:1-11
making me realize my lifestyle is not forgiven.
Then here comes Romans 14: 1-2,
where acceptance was made for me too.
You teach me more of Mark 12: 31,
where love should be given for everyone.
As the world is full of complexities,
Your thoughts still left a mystery.
As the love You shed on the cross,
Saving all needy across.
In the old times they call me cheerful.
Good words that makes the room wonderful.
In the present, culture gives us another meaning.
Words that would hurt someone's preening.
Is there a place in heaven?
Where I can sit right next to You?
Even my sexuality the world condemned,
Still doing good for the glory of You.

Gesture of Amity

Destiny Provokes

Born without any abundance,

    Raise with sound annoyance,

        Plan out change of a life ground —

            Fails when destiny spin her round and round.

Sometimes our eyes were not
enough to keep us with sight.
Sometimes the thickness of the cloud
wasn't enough to keep us with shed. More
of the thoughts our mind ponders.
More of desire my body wonder.
But to whom we should seek protection,
if life gave us pure desolation.

With plain mediocre,
work seems to be a fight for survival.
Good! If it was food fight.
Yet turn out it was a blood fight.

No one signed up for toxicity!
Yet when the air of hooligan escape
on a mouth of complainant,
there source of endless toxins been traced.

I was not your bet.
I was not your favored child.
Hence, here I am on top asking,
"Where are they now?"

Never eager to see you flourish and succeed.
Never imagine as well that I am busy cheering you up
while you are tearing me down.

Sound of emptiness fills my heart today.
I deem not to foster such curse.
However, the cycle keeps me weak
and the flow of tears beam in like a creek.

Helping's satisfaction brings you one piece of a puzzle.
Not to fix you but to fix them
while you give up a piece of you.

As drastic influence of authority can be
Some chose to infer harm to thee
Few leak the ink of despair
Never look to give a dare.
As drastic influence of authority can be
One never took the side of me
Throw my trust to the muddy road
Leaving thy corpse without any code.

Here comes a man with a torch
Offering a warmth cozy porch
With the words," On me you'll never scorch!"
Sometimes life gives us pain
To teach us how to gain
Same man with same pain give me sugar cane!

Unexpectedly

Two different souls collided unexpectedly
A mixture of order and chaos in harmony
Two different voices turned into a symphony
A universe conspired, orchestrated melody
It's a hand-made piece, deliberately made for me

You did not seek but earned my eternal devotion.
My intentions are pure; no signs of hesitation
Nuisance I might be, only yearns for your affection
You awaken my heart from its very long hibernation
You're the one I longed for, like the sweetest confection.

Wherever I am, I will always belong to you
Wished for a place in your heart that belongs to me, too
You are my safest haven, where my heart fell into.
In the ups and downs, will always be there to guide you.
Like a moon in the sky whenever you feel so blue
Under the blanket of stars, is where we will lay
Hold me in your arms tonight; don't ever go away
Even if life might give us lemons along the way.
I will always stay, until the day our hair turns gray.
Me and you, safe and sound, is every day what I pray.

Roque Jun Dilbert Tubaon

To my dearest love,

Words won't do it justice to express what I feel for you, but these mere words are the closest thing that brings me to heaven when I read them to you.

I am dumbfounded to know that we only met a few years ago, because it feels like I have known you my entire life and the past lives that we have lived through. I always wanted to touch you like a desert drought, longing for the rain, and I might have waited for too long, but not in vain.

You are the best thing that ever happened to me, and if I were to relive my life from the start, you're still the one I choose all over again, and till death makes us apart. You are like a sunlight that brightens up my day; you always wear those beautiful smiles and the look in your dreamy eyes that easily swept me away. I needed you in a heartbeat and like the very air I breathe. You came into my life and turned it upside down and you have shaken the foundation of my beliefs that I don't deserve better by proving me wrong. You loved me unconditionally and I realized you're the one that I have been waiting for too long. I know everything will not live forever and has an end, like this letter I created for you is about to come to its end, but my love for you will stay with you until the very end. Your love,

Roque Jun Dilbert Tubaon

Life is like your lawn
Wisely weed out the pawn
To make sure the safety of your queen
To safeguard a sure win!

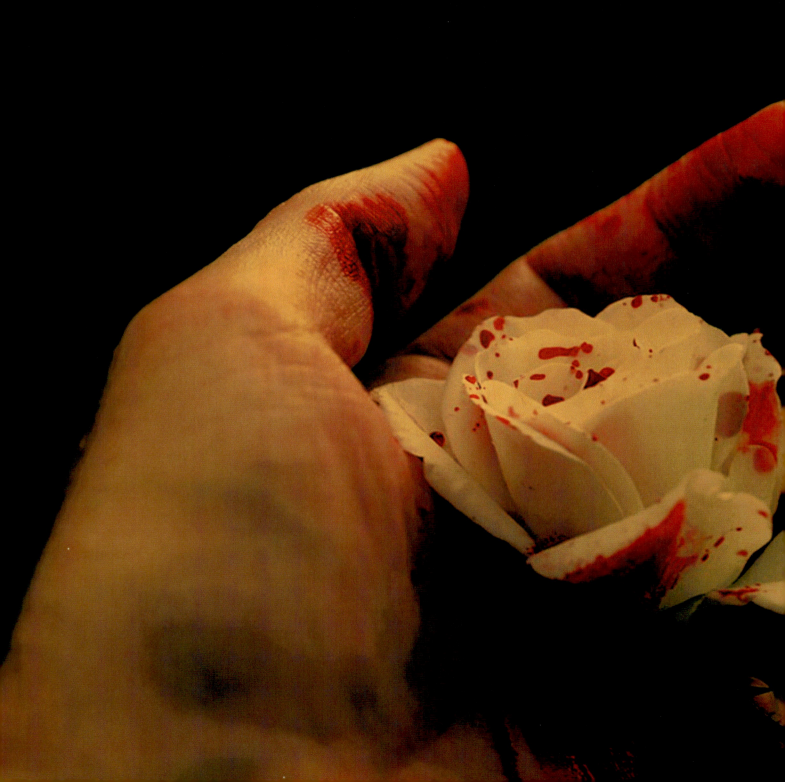

First

To realize, "You are my deepest yearning."
The idol whom made my heart capable of feeling,
Fate plays giant joke on the making –
Your heart speaks a different name.
As I was not acquainted with the happiness of love,
Here comes the pain that most describe.
Unfortunate that my first heartbeat is my first heartache.

From the First

It is just a matter of time
When the seed of my emotion
Finally flourish in your heart –
You will be mine.

Secretly, I planted moments
Concealed future plans
Shown you security
Safety and comfort with me.

Your heart is safe with me.
I won't let your past define our future.
I will be your total refuge
From the tormenting waves that might hit you.

You are my first
I was not.
You will be my last
Hoping I will be.

Stay

Spent ages avoiding to fall,
Flouting cares received to not feel
Covered my cemented heart with coil
Even things heat up to boil.

Here's a lady whom bravely spoke
borrowed a minute and poke.
Dropped all the task at hand
Wishing! I am just a bubble and gone.

The wall that I proudly built -
Wobble 'n teardown by your sound.
Not even a single swift of your hand
While I struggle to simply stand.

What whimsy did you bring?
To give my dying heart a ring.
What charm do you have?
To let me haste and grab.

To every start there must be an end
Even the found happiness in my pretend
As the clock speaks the truth –
You are not to be owned; neither to be bought.

So, the least I say,
"Here I gamble!"
Will you grant my way?
To finally- STAY?

Today you know my emotion
As I take the risk through a confession
Things get clearer that you can't be my possession
Even I offer you the crowd's veneration.
It is evident that you worship someone else
It doesn't take an inch of discouragement
as my heart melts
It doesn't stop me from feeling you
Although I am not your view.

Silly Woman

A silly woman full of doubts.
There I met with her lips pout!
She start listing things she complaints about
and here I am to contrast and shout!

She says, "I am not desired!"
I say, "Yes, you are!"
Desired by many eyes
Which you gave an ice!

She says, "I am not loved!"
I say, "Yes, you are!"
Loved by more than one
Who knows, it might be a band!

She says, "I want to be wanted!"
I say, "You are wanted!"
Wanted by some
Which by your voice came to a bright!

She says, "I want to be listened!"
I say, "You are being listened."
Listened to the point this poetry
Is created and wanted to cry!

Yet her eyes are set to only one.
While standing right beside her
is a great connection
Yet her ears are only for one voice
Leaving any scream a no choice.

What she did not know!

I felt drawn to her the moment I saw her tears,
Cursing inside! As the feeling flares.
She deserves the world not a goat.
She deserves a home and not just a coat.

She questions her appearance, "Oh, come on!"
Her eyes speaks softness saying, "Dream on!"
Her smile gives wonder and made misery gone.
Why cannot I just rush and kiss her
and to have this done?

Sadly, I cannot. Oh, silly me!
The friendship is at risk. So, let it be.
I will adore her from the distance
For I know, I got no chance.

Obvious Sign

As the thunder of emotional storm
Battles the unconventional norm
Comes the doubt of the conscience
As it was the opposite of convenience.

It was never a good disguise
Knowing one of your lies
To my surprise,
I am to pay the price!

Emaciated under the shackles of the mundane
Living life in a deranged world but trying to be sane
Going against the flow but caught up in a hurricane

-Roque Jun Dilbert Tubaon

Under the heat of the sun, there is a cold shoulder
Burning in my mind, but it gives me a cold shiver
Deafening silence like soundless thunder
No blood is spilled, but it does not mean the war is over

-Roque Jun Dilbert Tubaon

The Light Watch

Long dark stormy night!
The wrath of the sea hits my shore with its might.
The air utters curses on my metal plane.
The few decades stance with no complain.

I stand still to give a careful military watch.
I stand still to give you a shed to match.
Here I wonder. After few more decades!
Few more withering! Will I see you still on my facades?

After all the lonely night watch,
I grow weary while you comfortably dream.
After all the lonely night watch,
I drown with salt while you are safe with your cream.

Tonight, I felt the foundation wobble,
As I stay, still yet my legs felt like a bubble.
There is no more to gamble…
As the ground finally decides and tremble.

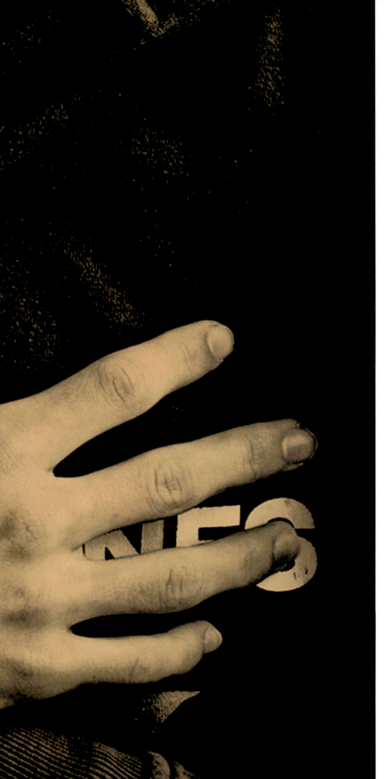

Days of the Week

As Monday jumps start the torment
Tuesday welcomes the familiar mourning.
Wednesday cheers the surviving
Thursday encourages the living.
Friday whispers and vindicating.
Saturday starts agonizing
Finally, Sunday bury the dying.

Contemporary Sonnet

Certain hour of the day; I would pray,
Hymn of despair in life's tangerine bay –
Would not lead to a soul's proud compunction
Nor to an ultimate desolation.
Certain hour of the day; I would say,
Judgement is not like hideous roll of hay –
Pick up every single silly stack,
Wisely store strong straws in shrouded sealed shack.
Don't wait for that certain time of the day,
Cherish every minute of your way,
Don't dawdle for pity thoughts if you may.
Try to be all smile it's a strong display,
Try to be all good to remove all gray,
Try to be all gentle and stop to prey.

Hopes

When we find something easy
We end up doing greasy.
When we jump for something safe
We end up as a bait.
When we try to reason,
We often lack conviction.
When we try to find connection,
it gives us more destruction.
Anger it brings to thy inner self.
Questions that grow on the shelf.
Mind that drowned in grief.
Tomorrow is a promise sheep
All the blubbering on thy sleep,
Finally, will be just a memory for keep.

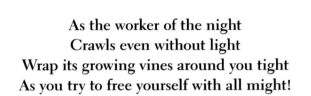

As the worker of the night
Crawls even without light
Wrap its growing vines around you tight
As you try to free yourself with all might!

The dark sky will not let you rest
Or even find refuge on anyone's chest
Not until the crawler brings you in the nest
All driven by his behest.

He can smell your fear
Even you cover gear
What more if he's in your ear!

The only way out is in.
Like the rest of your kin.
So save your last pin.

The wand lit on the swift dance of your arm,
Luminous colors rollick like a charm,
Combatant's eye caught amused but alarm,
Because he knew it will cause great harm.

Ordinary sky now filled with aurora,
Majestic like the spring's flora,
Mysterious like the famous Pandora,
Now the naked eye is witnessing the penumbra.

Beware when it hits the opponent!
Beware when you are the opponent!
Beware when spell flashes its components!

Realize that some colorful sight
Can greet us with such fright
When deception is full of light!

Half a decade gone too fast,
As if a strong time spell was cast.
Admit it! It was a dream –
'til the rainy morning come.

From the timeless addicting smile,
Here goes the sulky anwlite.
From the countless balmy clasp,
Here goes the loathing pinching.

You cry for retaliation
Yet I am the devisee.
Still I keep my close distance.

The sun come with complete numb.
Felt like in the process I am a bomb.
Here I explode, "I tried but no more!"

Printed in the United States
by Baker & Taylor Publisher Services